...ating Bl...s

EXCEPTIONAL IMAGES AND OBSERVATIONS

BY STAN TEKIELA

Adventure Publications, Inc.
Cambridge, MN

DEDICATION

For my father, whose love of nature sparked my passion for nature that still burns brightly today. Thank you, Dad.

ACKNOWLEDGMENTS

Special thanks to all bluebird recovery programs across this great nation. I also extend my appreciation to the Parks and Natural Resources Division of the City of Eden Prairie, Minnesota, where several images were taken for this book. Thanks to all people across the country who maintain bluebird trails, the site of many of my *Captivating Bluebirds* photographs.

Thanks also to Roberta Cvetnic and Carol Reinhart, who volunteered countless hours monitoring my bluebird trail of over 50 nest boxes. They were extremely helpful in sharing information over the years, and for that I am grateful. May you both have many bluebird years.

Special thanks to Joe Armstrong and Buck Huber for their help with several of the images.

Thanks to technical editor Dr. William J. Ehmann, Empire State College, State University of New York.

Cover photo by Stan Tekiela

All photos by Stan Tekiela except pp. 18, 58–59, 61, 84, 101, 128–129, 133 and 134 by Maslowski Wildlife Productions, pg. 135 by Michael L. Smith and pg. 125 by Jim Zipp. All photos were taken in the wild except for one, which was taken under a controlled condition.

Edited by Sandy Livoti

Cover and book design by Jonathan Norberg

TABLE OF CONTENTS

Bluebirds are easy to love. They possess all the ingredients to enthrall a bird watcher—an azure coat of blue, a warm, rich red breast and a song so soft and cheerful that you never tire of hearing it. Bluebirds are captivating songbirds that are tolerant of humans. They take up residency in birdhouses that we provide or build nests near us, in tree cavities close to the ground. They show little fear of people and readily come to feeding stations in our yards. What more could you ask of a wonderful little bird?

FIRST SIGHTINGS

When the colonists first came to North America, the
Eastern Bluebird stood out among the birds that greeted
the settlers. In those days it was called the Blew Bird. This
name was given to it in the early 1700s by Mark Catesby,
an English artist who produced one of the first field guides,
the two-volume Natural History of Carolina, Florida, and
the Bahama Islands, which described and illustrated the
never-before discovered native birds of America, including
the bluebird.

The early immigrants had never seen a bluebird prior to their arrival here because all bluebird species in the world—a total of three—occur only in North America. The colonists referred to the bluebird as a blue robin since it appeared similar to the European Robin, an Old World bird. The resemblance is not mere coincidence. The bluebird and European Robin are both members of Turdidae, which is the scientific family name for the Thrush family—a group of songbirds that consists of over 175 species worldwide.

THE THRUSH FAMILY

Other Thrush family members include the American Robin,
Veery and Swainson's Thrush. In western states we see the
Townsend's Solitaire and Varied Thrush. Most of these
birds share some common characteristics such as long legs
for hopping or running, plump round bodies, short narrow
bills for grabbing insects, large dark eyes, earth-tone feathers
and, except for bluebirds and adult robins, spotted chests.
Interestingly, both bluebirds and robins also have spotted
chests as juveniles. In general, they all hunt on the ground
or drop to the ground from a low perch to snatch prey.
Sometimes bluebirds will chase flying insects, snatching them
out of the air before landing to eat. Most thrush species,
including bluebirds, are migrators, spending winters in
warmer climates.

Bluebirds are also grouped with other songbirds in a huge order of birds called Passeriformes. Passeriformes include more than half of the world's bird species. Most of these birds have a well-developed voice box called a syrinx, which enables them to sing. Bluebird males do the singing, but unlike other birds, they don't open their mouths when in song.

ORIGINS OF THE SPECIES

The songbird evolved about 30 million years ago. Over time, it diversified into families such as thrushes, thrashers, warblers and sparrows. Although molecular analysis suggests that all bluebirds branched away from a common ancestor about 2.5 million years ago, their species are relatively recent when compared with others in the bird world that date back millions of years. The bluebird fossil record dates back about 10,000 years, with a few fossilized remains coming from Florida and Illinois. Other bluebird remains excavated in New Mexico date back 12,500–25,000 years.

LIFE SPAN

While research exists on bluebird ancestry, there are few studies on bluebird life span. One 1907 report mentions a captive bluebird living 10 years, but most reports on wild bird life span estimate 6–7 years. The best estimate is that on average, bluebirds live 3–8 years, with some individuals making it to 10 years of age. Due to the rigors of nature, approximately 20 percent of eggs laid don't hatch and about 15 percent of hatchlings fail to leave the nest, or fledge. Overall nest success for bluebirds is in the 70 percent range. Once the young leave the nest, their rate of survival is around 50 percent for the first year. After that, the survival rate goes up and remains stable.

Western Bluebird

Mountain Bluebird

There are three bluebird species in the United States. Known simply as Eastern Bluebird, Western Bluebird and Mountain Bluebird, they are named for their ranges.

Eastern Bluebirds occur throughout the eastern half of the country and up into southeastern and south central Canada.

Western Bluebirds are mainly found in southwestern states, but their range extends through California, Oregon, Washington and into southwestern Canada.

Mountain Bluebirds are more widespread than Western Bluebirds, occurring throughout the mountainous western half of the United States, reaching well into western Canada and farther north into central Alaska.

Each species is also found in Mexico, but Mountain Bluebirds are seen there only after they migrate south for the winter.

Eastern Bluebird

The Eastern Bluebird is used for nearly all bluebird studies, but some reports have stated that interbreeding occurs among the three species where ranges overlap. Interbreeding is uncommon, however, and does not result in hybrid offspring.

Bergmann's rule states that animals in cold northern climates are larger than the same species in warm southern climates, but this is not evident for bluebirds. Eastern Bluebirds vary only slightly in size and appearance throughout their range. Those in southwestern states, such as Arizona, and northern Mexico are not as vibrant blue as their counterparts along the East Coast. Bluebirds in northern states have just slightly shorter bills than those residing in Florida.

WHITE BLUEBIRDS

Occasionally, a bluebird hatches looking different from its siblings due to a defect in the specialized cells within feathers that make a bluebird blue. This condition, called leucism, sometimes produces partly white plumage and other times results in just a few white feathers or an all-white bird. Leucism is different from albinism. Leucistic birds have dark eyes and many degrees of white unlike albino birds, which always have pink eyes and an entire coat of pure white feathers.

Since early settlement times, the Eastern Bluebird
has had other common names such as American
Bluebird, Red-breasted Bluebird and Blue
Redbreast. The name "Eastern Bluebird" probably
became preferred since it describes both location
and color. The same holds true for the Western and
Mountain Bluebirds, although Mountain Bluebirds
also occur in areas that are not mountainous.

The Eastern Bluebird's first scientific name, *Motacilla sialis*, was given by Swedish biologist Carolus Linnaeus in 1758. He chose the genus *Motacilla* because he felt bluebirds were closely related to wagtails, a group of semi-colorful birds found in Europe and Asia. In 1827, when English naturalist William Swainson realized that Eastern Bluebirds were closely related to robins, not wagtails, he created a new genus for them by replacing the last letter of the species name *sialis* to create a new genus, *Sialia*. This changed the scientific name of the Eastern Bluebird to *Sialia sialis*. The name *sialis* is a Greek word that means a "kind of bird," but this falls far short in describing such a spectacular creature.

Western and Mountain Bluebirds are also in the same genus. The Western Bluebird's scientific name, *Sialia mexicana*, includes a reference to another part of its range, which extends deep into Mexico.

The scientific name of the Mountain Bluebird is *Sialia currucoides*. Its species name is similar to *curruca*, a species of Old World warbler. Thus, *Sialia currucoides*, meaning "looks like the Lesser Whitethroat," refers to a bird not found in North America.

Groups of birds sometimes develop slightly different characteristics relative to the region in which they live. When this occurs in a bird species that has a broad geographical distribution, ornithologists divide the species into other groups called subspecies. This is accomplished simply by adding a third name after the genus and species names.

There are no known subspecies for the Mountain Bluebird, seven known subspecies for the Western Bluebird and eight for the Eastern Bluebird, *Sialia sialis*. *Sialia sialis sialis* is found in the eastern United States, southern Canada and northeastern Mexico. *Sialia sialis grata* is seen in central and southern Florida. *Sialia sialis fulva* occurs in southern Arizona and also Mexico. *Sialia sialis bermudensis* is in Bermuda. *Sialia sialis nidificans* occurs on the eastern coast of Mexico. *Sialia sialis guatemalae* is found in southern Mexico and Guatemala. *Sialia sialis caribaea* occurs in Nicaragua and eastern Honduras. *Sialia sialis meridionalis* is seen in Honduras and northern El Salvador and Nicaragua.

Size and plumage differences among Eastern Bluebird subspecies are generally minor and go unnoticed by casual observers. Also, the ranges of some subspecies overlap, obscuring the slight distinctions even further.

Eastern Bluebird populations in America have gone up and down like a roller coaster over the past two centuries. When European settlers first arrived in the late 1700s, Eastern Bluebirds were fairly uncommon on the East Coast. Deciduous forest covered nearly half of the eastern United States instead of the open habitats that bluebirds prefer. In the 1800s, people moved westward, clearing millions of forested acres for farming and lumber and creating fields, prairies and meadows. By the late 1800s and early 1900s, Eastern Bluebirds were thriving in the new open spaces, and their numbers soared to an all-time high.

Around this time, several events occurred that severely impacted Eastern Bluebird populations. Bluebirds are secondary cavity nesters. This means they nest in cavities, but cannot excavate their own. A major influence on the nesting success of bluebirds was the introduction of other cavity-nesting species. New immigrants imported House Sparrows and European Starlings for sentimental reasons, mostly as reminders of home. These birds are more aggressive at defending or obtaining a cavity, and bluebirds simply lost the competition for the limited supply of natural cavities and vacant woodpecker homes.

The availability of woodpecker homes is vital because bluebirds rely on woodpeckers to excavate cavities for them. When the forests disappeared, so did woodpecker habitat. Farmers used small tree trunks and large branches from cleared forests to construct fence posts. With few trees left for nesting, fence posts became the most common place for woodpeckers to excavate. After the woodpeckers nested and moved out, bluebirds moved in. These residents were welcomed by farmers because they ate many destructive insects around the farmlands.

The invention of the metal fence post was a major factor in the decline of bluebirds. As the wooden posts rotted, they were replaced by metal posts, which offered no nesting opportunities for woodpeckers or bluebirds.

Another modern invention, the gas-powered chain saw, is often blamed for contributing to the bluebird's downward spiral. Patented and developed in 1926 and mass-produced in 1929, the chain saw made cutting dead wood and land clearing more efficient. Dead trees and tree limbs that might have decomposed naturally were felled in record numbers from the 1930s to the 1950s and, with that, the loss of habitat for woodpeckers and, in turn, bluebirds.

Pesticide and insecticide use also played a role in dwindling bluebird populations. After World War II, pesticide use increased sharply as U.S. farmers endeavored to feed the growing human population. In 1939, DDT was introduced and quickly became the most widely used pesticide in the country and the world. By the 1960s, it was discovered that DDT was preventing many bird species from reproducing and its use was banned in the United States. Other pesticide use had increased and still continues today—currently about 2.5 million tons of industrial pesticides are used annually. Bluebirds feed mainly on ground-dwelling insects, which, when suffering from the effects of insecticides, are easily caught. With each tainted insect eaten, toxic chemicals increase in the bird's system. This eventually kills the bird or severely impacts its reproduction.

DOMESTIC PREDATORS

Domestic cats and dogs, and vehicles have reduced Eastern Bluebird populations as well. Unattended pet cats, barnyard mousers and stray felines take a huge toll on all bird species including the bluebird. The same is true for dogs that are permitted to run wild. As traffic and speed limits increased, instances of bluebirds being hit and killed by cars also grew. In open habitat, more bluebird deaths occur at roadsides, where bluebirds often take flight to snatch an insect.

Recognition of the Eastern Bluebird's plight became evident from the 1950s to the 1970s. In regions east of the Mississippi River, bluebirds were at record lows. The bluebird had been extirpated—completely eliminated—in many areas and across entire states. It was estimated that, sadly, upward of 90 percent of the total bluebird population was gone.

Individuals and organizations in eastern states noticing the decline started developing plans for recovery. In 1970, all three bluebird species were added to the Audubon Society's Blue List, which records species of birds that are declining in numbers. By 1978, the North American Bluebird Society formed. This brought bluebird enthusiasts together from across the nation and unified their efforts to save all bluebird species.

People began fashioning wooden nest boxes to replicate natural cavities and started placing them in areas where small populations still existed. With the success of nest boxes, word spread and more boxes were constructed and installed. As a result, bluebird populations started to increase across America.

There are thousands of individuals and organizations from coast to coast maintaining countless bluebird nest boxes. Many bluebird enthusiasts have 10 to over 100 nest boxes strung along suitable habitats. These networks of boxes are called bluebird trails. An owner monitors a trail, visiting each nest box once a week to document nesting activity, evict House Sparrows and make repairs. Having a bluebird trail is a great responsibility that offers heart-warming rewards—watching and helping these beloved birds and their babies thrive.

The recovery of the bluebird has been nothing short of amazing. In most areas where bluebirds had ceased to exist, their cheery song is now heard. In other areas where bluebirds never lived, they have moved in and are doing well. Bluebirds still are not found in all suitable habitats since the lack of nest cavities remains the limiting factor in the expansion of the species. In suburban areas, where there aren't enough natural cavities for bluebirds to use, the only way for the birds to flourish is with the installation of nest boxes.

Simply putting up some bluebird boxes in yards or local parks is not a quick and easy way to help bluebirds. This can be detrimental to bluebirds if the style or placement of the box is not carefully considered. There are many other species of birds that will take up residency in a nest box meant for bluebirds. In fact, if nest boxes are not put up in the correct manner, they will only serve to encourage other species.

Bluebird recovery was well documented by data provided in the Christmas Bird Count (CBC), coordinated by the National Audubon Society. Since 1900, the CBC has been gathering actual numbers of individual birds seen during the same 3-week period in December across the United States. Thousands of volunteers went forth with one mission—to count all birds in a well-defined geographical area. With over 100 years of data, it was easy to chart the recovery of the bluebird. Since the mid-70s, their numbers have increased every year.

Periodically, bluebird populations have dropped drastically. These population crashes almost always were related to severe winter weather and freak ice storms in spring, when the birds are most vulnerable. Crashes occurring every 10–15 years usually affected only local populations. Recovery in these pockets comes fairly quickly, often within a couple years. In the late 1970s, harsh winters in some southern states caused bluebird population crashes there, as did storms in 1911–12, 1939–40 and 1957–58. Short-term declines such as these are natural cycles and, fortunately, have no long-term effect.

THE FUTURE

The future of the bluebird is as bright as its beauty. There are thousands of individuals and organizations dedicated to the preservation and propagation of the species, and more join in recovery efforts every year. Through education and well-managed trails, the bluebird should never see another time when its populations struggle again.

All bluebird males have vivid blue feathers. Female bluebirds are dull gray with just a hint of blue in the tail and wings. Distinct color differences such as these between male and female birds within a species is called sexual dimorphism or dichromatism. Being sexually dimorphic sets the bluebird apart from the Wood Thrush, Hermit Thrush and other Thrush family species in which the male and female look identical or nearly so.

The male Eastern Bluebird has a bright blue head, back, tail and wings. It sports a rich, rusty red chest, body, rump and flanks, which contrast with its white belly.

When it comes to blue, the female Eastern Bluebird is a mere shadow of the brilliant male. Even her rusty chest is dull, with only half the color intensity of the male. Some believe this helps reduce the visibility of the female while she is incubating—although since the nest is concealed by the darkness of the cavity, the color of her feathers shouldn't make a difference. One study of Northern Cardinals showed that the males, which are much brighter red than female cardinals, were disproportionately killed by hawks. If bright feathers attract hawks, perhaps that explains why the feathers of female bluebirds are dull.

UNUSUAL FEATHERS

Birds the size and shape of bluebirds have roughly 2,500 feathers during summer. In fall and winter they can have up to one-third more feathers, which are gained during molting. Molting is the process of shedding old feathers and growing new ones, usually in an orderly pattern and not all over simultaneously. Most birds molt twice each year, once from fall to early winter, when extra feathers are added for warmth, and again from late winter to early spring, when winter feathers are replaced with newer, fewer feathers.

In summer, when they are not molting, bluebirds can lose up to a third more of their feather mass as the tips and edges wear away. This occurs during everyday activities such as flying, going in and out of the nest cavity, rubbing against branches and catching insects.

PLUMAGE FINERY

The feathers of a male bluebird are remarkable in uniqueness and design. Only 2 percent of North American bird species have blue feathers. Most birds have black, gray, brown, yellow or red feathers that contain pigments of the same colors. Bluebird feathers, however, do not have blue pigment. In fact, there is no blue pigment in the blue feathers of any bird worldwide.

The blue color in feathers is caused by scattered light waves in feather cells. Under a microscope, these unique light-scattering cells show a dark pigment sandwiched between two layers of hollow, tubular cells. When light enters the cell, the pigment absorbs most wavelengths of light. The remaining light— blue light—is scattered and reflected back to our eyes, resulting in an optical illusion that makes the feathers appear blue. The brightness and intensity of blue changes with the amount of sunlight and time of day. On cloudy days or when the sun is low in the sky, the blue is less intense. The blue appearance is most intense under direct sun at midday.

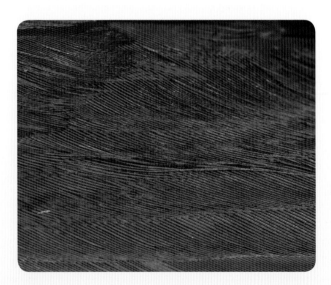

The dull feathers of sexually dimorphic female birds are thought to be for camouflage, as protection against predators during nesting and incubation. If this is true, however, a female bluebird shouldn't need dull plumage since the darkness of the nest box or cavity will hide even bright colors. Besides, brighter, nondimorphic females, such as robins, use open nests. With duller females nesting in dark cavities, brighter females sitting in open nests and all species thriving, our conclusion about camouflage plumage appears to need more study.

Exceptional eyesight is essential for bluebirds, just as it is for most other birds. Bluebirds are expert insect hunters mainly because of their excellent vision. They will often perch on a branch over open ground and move their heads quickly from side to side, looking for any movement. An insect is relatively safe if it doesn't move, but once it does, the bluebird locks onto its location and swiftly flies or drops to the ground to grab it.

A bluebird's eyes are very large relative to its head—an indication of just how important eyes are to the species. With eyes located on the sides, the bluebird has excellent side vision and good vision to the front. Only about 10–20 percent of the vision from each eye overlaps in front, allowing for some stereoscopic vision and good depth perception. Eyes on the sides of the head also allows for some vision to the rear of the bird, which helps when watching for predators.

Similar to other members of the Thrush family, the bluebird will often turn and cock its head. This maneuver points one eye directly at an object—it doesn't aid in hearing, a common misconception. Bluebirds have the ability to concentrate their vision or see out of one eye at a time. Turning or cocking the head facilitates this one-eyed approach to viewing the world around them.

The bill, or beak, of a bluebird does exactly what is needed to capture food and clean feathers. It's not overly large, like the bill of a Bald Eagle, and it's not as dainty as the beak of a Pine Siskin. A bluebird's bill is medium to short and rather narrow—perfect for catching insects or carrying food back to the nest.

A bluebird often uses its bill to kill (dispatch) a large insect for a meal. Holding the bug in its bill, the bird repeatedly hits the prey against a branch or other hard surface. Sometimes it "chews" an insect to death by moving the prey back and forth in its bill in a chewing fashion. The prey is either eaten or flown to the nest to be fed to the young.

At the base of the bill are two holes, which are nostrils. The sense of smell is greatly reduced in bluebirds and is not used to help locate food. Air is simply taken in through the nostrils and expelled for breathing and singing.

EAR APPEAL

As songbirds, it makes sense for bluebirds to have excellent hearing—and they do. A bluebird's ears are small, located beneath the feathers slightly below and behind the eyes. Studies show that males with the most complete and loudest songs attract the most females. The male's song, along with his blue feathers, is a way for a bluebird suitor to say, "Hey, consider me! I'm a healthy male who can provide for a family." Females listen for males singing their courtship song in spring, while males listen for competing males and their songs.

Male bluebirds have one of the most beautiful songs in the bird world. While other thrushes are known for some of the loudest, most complex and penetrating songs, the bluebird's song is more like a lullaby. It is a soft, sweet warble that is extremely pleasant to hear.

Most songbirds perch high on a favorite perch, tilt their heads back, open their beaks and belt out their song. Bluebirds sit on prominent perches in their territory, but they don't tilt their heads back and you won't see them open their beaks widely during song like a cardinal or blue jay. It is almost as if they are suppressing their singing so only their loved ones can hear it.

The song is often described as several alternating refrains in a rising pitch, as if the bird may be asking and answering, "Ayo ala looee? Alee ay lalo leeo!" Others say it sounds more like "chiti WEEW wewidoo" or "jeew wiwi." However you hear it, you are sure to be impressed by the lilting melody.

Studies of bluebird songs show that males sing over 20 different phrases, or micro songs, each lasting only 1–2 seconds and consisting of just a few notes. Micro songs are strung together with a very brief, almost undetectable pause between the songs. Males use micro songs in many combinations, often repeating a phrase several times before moving to another set. These songs are often interrupted with a series of louder, staccato notes called chattering calls. Chattering calls are usually seen as an aggressive component of a bluebird's overall song. Chattering by itself is sometimes described as an angry call and usually is given when predators or other threats enter a male's territory or approach the nest cavity.

TERRITORIAL AND INTIMATE SONGS

Predawn is when bluebird males sing most of their territorial songs. Unlike cardinals, bluebirds don't counter-sing—singing songs back and forth to each other from different territories. Instead, males move to the edge of their territories and sing up to 15 different songs per minute. They may alternate 3–4 songs, starting each group differently from the previous round.

Males also sing very soft secondary songs. These intimate songs are meant just for the mate and serve to strengthen the pair bond. The male usually sings these songs in close proximity to the female, as if whispering sweet-nothings in her ear. It is thought that sometimes female bluebirds also sing, but this is not well documented.

Like all other birds, bluebirds like to bathe. They will take a bath in just about any shallow water source such as a birdbath, pond edge, stream or even a puddle in a driveway after rain. A bluebird usually starts a bath by lowering its head and breast into the water. Then, after shaking its head and beating the water's surface with its wings, the bird rises up from the water—only to dunk its belly and rump back in, all the while spreading its tail feathers and doing a bluebird version of the funky chicken dance.

SUNBATHING

Sometimes bluebirds enjoy a sunbath. A bird crouching down, back toward the sun, with wings spread and feathers raised on its head and back, is allowing sunlight to penetrate deeply into its feathers. It is thought this helps reduce mites and ticks, which prefer dark places, but perhaps it is just simply enjoyable.

ANTING

Another unusual behavior of bluebirds is called anting. A bird is anting when it lands at an ant mound and crouches down with wings and tail spread, allowing ants to crawl onto its feathers. The theory is that ants attack the bird in defense of their home. When ants bite the bird's feathers, they release formic acid. While this chemical doesn't bother the bird, it presumably repels tiny insects and helps rid pests from the feathers. Anting and sunbathing are common behaviors not only in bluebirds, but in other bird species as well.

Cleaning and straightening feathers, or preening, is a vital part of any bird's day. Not only do feathers enable a bird to fly, their physical condition affects a bird's very life. Feathers provide warmth during cold, wet weather and protection from the scorching sun on hot days. In addition, most male birds display sanitary, well-groomed feathers to advertise they are healthy and worthy of mating. This is one case where "clothing" really does make a difference—you might say a bird is not a bird without its feathers!

Preening occurs any time a feather is out of place. In the same way a scratch needs to be itched, a feather needs to be preened. The bird gently draws its beak through a misaligned feather, straightening it into position. Any feather that can be reached will be preened. Places that can't be preened with the bill, such as the top of the head, are scratched with the foot and combed with the toes.

Preening often occurs after bathing. A wet bluebird will fly to a perch, where it shakes, fluffs and rearranges its feathers for 30 seconds to several minutes. The tiny down feathers next to its body are individually preened, and tail and wing feathers are pulled through the bill, zipping together any disheveled sections. Preening also includes much tail wagging and wing shaking. Finally, using specialized muscles, the bird fluffs all its feathers and gives a total body shake before getting back to other activities.

WHAT'S FOR LUNCH?

The bluebird hunts mainly by perching on a branch
or tall object and watching for moving insects. After
spotting one, the bluebird quickly flies down and
"pounces" on the bug. Small insects are eaten on the
spot, but a large insect is usually carried to a branch,
where it is beaten against the perch until subdued.
A bluebird will "chew" a large bug by moving the
prey back and forth in its bill in a chewing fashion.
Bluebirds "chew" noxious Monarch caterpillars until
they become completely flat, squeezing most of the
harmful innards out at the ends. It seems a good way to
deal with a possibly toxic lunch.

It's a wonderful sign of spring when the bluebirds
return. But while bluebirds do migrate, they are not
true migrators—they have no consistent, seasonal
pattern of migration such as flying long distances to
southern locations and returning in spring. Bluebirds
in northern states usually don't fly too far south,
and those in most central and southern parts of the
country don't migrate at all. Non-migrators joined
by northern migrants often form winter flocks and
remain together until it is nearly spring.

Bluebirds are believed to be diurnal migrants, usually migrating during the day. This is unlike most other songbirds, which migrate at night. Males often arrive at their destinations before the females; occasionally they arrive together. Several studies involving adult bluebirds with numbered leg bands showed 30–50 percent returned to the nest site of the previous year. Juvenile Eastern Bluebirds tend to migrate separately from the adults and may stay together all winter before heading north as a group.

Mountain Bluebirds may have the longest migration of the three bluebird species, since those in Alaska and Canada migrate thousands of miles to Arizona, New Mexico and Mexico. Some Mountain Bluebirds in the Colorado and California mountains simply move down from the high country to lower, warmer elevations.

Western Bluebirds in Washington and Oregon move to the coast and down to California to spend the winter. In many other locations, these birds are non-migrators.

In areas where the ranges of Mountain and Western Bluebirds overlap, the birds often migrate at the same time. Where Eastern and Mountain Bluebird ranges overlap, Mountain Bluebirds arrive first, up to 2 weeks ahead in spring. It appears that Mountain Bluebirds are the hardiest of the bluebird species, able to withstand colder weather the best.

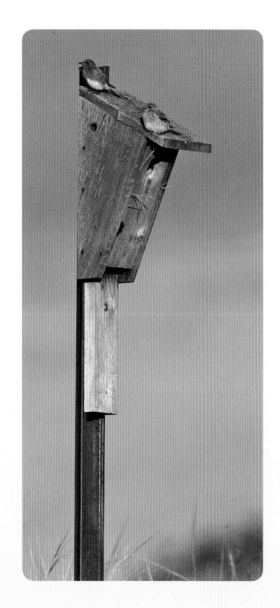

SPRING ARRIVAL

Most bluebirds start to arrive at breeding grounds in late March in northern states and around mid-February in the South. Bluebirds may come individually, in small groups or occasionally in large flocks. When weather is good, individuals start to pair up, scout prospective cavities and maybe even bring in dried grass to build a nest. Bluebirds may retreat from the area temporarily to find food and refuge if the weather turns bad.

It is not uncommon for some bluebird pairs to begin or complete a nest—usually the first nest of the year—only to leave or abandon it. While this behavior is common in cardinals, finches and many other songbird species, the reason for it is unknown.

Bluebird territories vary in size and shape, depending on habitat and available food. A territory with suitable man-made or natural nest cavities and a sufficient food supply, such as insects and berries, can be as small as 2–3 acres. Territories providing less food might be as large as 5 acres. Most bluebirds, especially those living on bluebird trails, nest 100 yards or more apart. Other nests can be as close as 100 feet. In all cases, bluebirds defend their territories against neighboring bluebirds and any other threats. Bluebirds with bluebird neighbors usually hunt within their territories. Bluebirds without bluebird neighbors often roam up to a quarter mile in search of food.

Males establish territories, with the process beginning immediately after they arrive. Deciding on a location is the first thing to do—often it is near the previous year's nest or the birthplace. After checking out a territory, a male will start singing from prominent perches. Then, flying along the edges of the domain, he will go from perch to perch, singing. Hard lines between territories are not drawn until a neighboring male has been sufficiently challenged. When two males vie for the same territory, the dominant or older male usually prevails. After territories are established, males begin to sing and display to attract a mate.

HOME DEFENSE

A male and female defend their territory together, but in different ways and for different reasons. While the male defends the entire area, the female protects the nest site and immediate area. The male defends against other males, but allows females to enter for mating. The female welcomes males for mating, but chases out other females to prevent them from mating with her male and dumping their eggs in her nest.

Territories are defended only during breeding season. Sometimes bluebirds will defend a territory into autumn, well after the last baby bird has left the nest. These cases, however, are most likely just the result of overactive hormones.

After a male establishes a territory, his next priority is to attract a mate with courting songs and displays. First, he perches on prominent places in his territory and sings a loud song. This is a short attraction song that may be repeated up to 30 times a minute. While singing, the male stays attentive, scanning the territory for an approaching female, often moving to another perch to start the song again. Sometimes he will continue to sing in flight as he flies from perch to perch.

FLIGHT DISPLAYS

When a female enters his territory, the male communicates more personally. Even if the female is his previous mate, he performs flight displays to call even more attention to himself. Flight displays include stalling in flight with deep butterfly-like wing beats.

Once the male has caught the female's eye, he flies to the nest cavity to wing wave—a flashy behavior that really gets her attention. Depending on her position, he will use one or both wings to do this. If she is to the right, he waves his left wing so the entire blue surface is visible to her, and vice versa when she is on his left. Often he will crouch, facing away from her to show his blue back and the entire surface of both upper wings. Eventually, he goes to the cavity entrance and clings to the opening.

Meantime, the female has landed on the nest box or may have perched nearby to watch. Now the male repeatedly pokes his head through the entrance hole or enters the cavity. If nothing entices her to inspect the interior, he will try wing waving again.

Usually when a female enters the cavity, it is good sign the birds will pair and nest. It's an even better clue if both birds enter the cavity. While this doesn't guarantee the cavity will be used, it is a great indication of familial things to come.

When a female shows no interest in a cavity, the male performs more flight displays and wing waves or just moves to another cavity and starts over again. As a last resort, he will fly off to catch a bug or two and return to feed her. This often seals the deal, and the pair prepares for mating and nest construction.

Courtship continues from one to many days. More experienced birds are faster at acquiring mates. First-timers are often tentative and take longer.

MATE-FEEDING

Once the pair bond is established, it is constantly reinforced by a special behavior called mate-feeding. In mate-feeding, a male captures caterpillars, grasshoppers or whatever delicious morsels are available and feeds them to his female. The female usually squats, spreads her wings slightly and quivers while opening her beak in anticipation of food. This resembles the posture of young bluebirds begging for food. Some believe this ritual demonstrates to the female how well the male is going to provide for their young.

Some pairs will mate-feed often. In others the occurrence is less frequent, and in still others it does not take place at all. In fact, it appears that some entire populations mate-feed, while other populations do not.

During this time, a pair will fly around their territory, hunting and exchanging soft call notes to keep in contact with each other. The male may even sing a soft song to his mate, but it is so quiet that you need to be very close to him to hear it. Soft songs are thought to strengthen the pair bond, not to attract another female—or worse, a predator or competing male.

MATING AFFAIRS

Despite the showy behaviors, soft calling and mate-feeding going on, bluebird romances apparently aren't all roses. While most bluebirds have a traditional coupling of one male and one female (monogamous), there are many instances of one male attending two females in his territory. If the first female doesn't drive off a second female her mate attracts, the male will court and mate both females. Usually the second female builds her own nest in a separate cavity, but there have been cases where two females have laid their eggs in one nest and both mothers have incubated the eggs at the same time!

There are also cases where two males have attended one female. Apparently these males shared their territories as well as their one mate. Usually baby birds with two male parents have no problems being fed since both fathers bring in the food.

Bluebirds have been known to nest in a variety of surprising places. Some have nested in the mud nests of swallows. Others have made their homes in large cracks or crevices in soil. Still others have settled in gravel mines, old mailboxes, broken light fixtures, drain pipe openings and other low places with some kind of cavity. The best locations for bluebird nests, however, are in open fields, fencerows, prairies, parks and yards with large open areas since these are excellent places for hunting insects.

Interestingly, studies show that bluebirds hatching in nest boxes will choose similar style nest boxes when they become adults and are nesting. For example, bluebirds that hatch in Peterson-style boxes favor Peterson-style boxes to nest in during their breeding season. Conversely, bluebirds hatching in natural cavities prefer similar natural cavities for nesting when the time comes for them to breed.

CAVITY NESTING

Forty bird species in North America nest in cavities. Some are primary cavity nesters, excavating their own cavities. Others, such as bluebirds, are secondary cavity nesters. Woodpeckers are primary cavity nesters, with nearly all species excavating cavities in trees. Most use the cavity to incubate eggs and raise young only once. After their young leave the nest, the abandoned cavity becomes available for bluebirds or other secondary cavity nesters. Bluebirds will use a tree cavity for as long as the tree or branch lasts.

Before humans started building nest boxes, bluebirds
were completely dependent on woodpeckers and,
to a much lesser extent, natural cavities in trees
for nesting opportunities. Today the majority of
all bluebirds nest in boxes constructed by people.
Man-made nest boxes have entrance holes small
enough to keep out certain bird competitors and
predators. They generally are safer, drier, better
ventilated and more stable than woodpecker or
natural cavities. Where there are no trees or existing
cavities, bluebird populations are completely
dependent on nest boxes for raising families.

After setting up a territory, the male selects potential nest cavities for his mate. The female chooses her favorite and is the sole builder of the nest. Sometimes, perhaps to stimulate the female into starting construction, a male will bring small amounts of nesting material to the cavity. Occasionally he will go into the cavity and rearrange the material or remove small amounts. Nests are usually made with dried grass, but females will use whatever material is most abundant such as pine needles. Nests have also been constructed with plant stalks, roots and other small, natural materials.

Nests are in the shape of a cup or small bowl. The female gathers and deposits mouthfuls of dried grass into the cavity and arranges it into the general desired shape. Then, using her chest and belly, she forms the inside of the cup. Often this is lined with finer grass to make it softer for the chicks.

Nest construction lasts from one to several days, depending on the female's ability, experience, available nesting materials, weather and more. Some nests are shallow, having barely enough grass to cover the bottom of the cavity. Others are sturdy, with tall sides and a thick floor. Occasionally Tree Swallows barge in, add a few feathers, take over the nest and evict the bluebirds. In the photo on the right, the lone bluebird egg did not hatch with the swallow eggs. This is a typical outcome, probably due to lost incubation time during takeover. When eviction fails, bluebirds keep the feathers in place and continue their nesting duties.

Sometimes, despite the persistent efforts of the male, a female won't build a nest. When bluebird observers notice this, some people gather fine, dried grass and form a little nest inside the cavity. Others put small amounts of dried grass on the roof of the box for the female to find and use. Perhaps the bird will build her nest without the help of impatient humans, but many swear by this method of "helping" the process along.

EGG LAYING

Bluebirds usually lay 4–5 eggs. Like all other birds, female bluebirds lay only a single egg per day. This means if a mother bluebird is laying 5 eggs, she will take 5 days to do it. Each egg lies in the nest uncovered and unattended until the last egg is laid. In warm weather, before the mother starts incubating, the first eggs laid may begin developing and get a head start due to the interior heat of the nest box.

Although Eastern Bluebirds usually lay 4–5 eggs, they have an average range of 3–6. Some Eastern Bluebird nests have contained up to 9–10 eggs, but this is uncommon and may be the result of two females laying eggs in the same nest cavity. Like Eastern Bluebirds, Mountain Bluebirds often produce 4–5 eggs, but have a range of 2–6. Western Bluebirds also have a range of 2–6, but typically lay 5 eggs.

Eggs are usually light blue, but some females lay white eggs. The reason for these colorless eggs is usually the result of a lack of specific nutrition in the mother. Young birds from white eggs are perfectly healthy and hatch at the same rate as those from blue eggs. Sometimes a very large blue egg is found in a nest; other times an extremely small egg is produced. While these occurrences are uncommon, the eggs are almost always infertile and do not hatch.

BROOD PATCH

To transfer sufficient heat to the eggs during incubation, female bluebirds lose the inner down feathers closest to the body on the belly and lower chest. The resulting bare spot of skin is called a brood patch. A brood patch becomes highly vascularized with many arteries and veins carrying warm blood at a temperature of about 97°F—a perfect heat for warming eggs. When a female is not incubating, the brood patch is hidden, covered by the larger contour feathers that give the bird its shape and color. After the breeding season, feathers in the brood patch area grow back. Male bluebirds do not develop a brood patch.

EGG CARE

The female bluebird does all of the incubation full-time, covering the eggs with her warm brood patch nearly nonstop during the day and continuously at night. During the day, the female takes several breaks to stretch her wings, feed, defecate and drink. She may leave the eggs several times on warm days for up to several hours each time. On cold days she may not leave at all. Eggs can withstand much cooling, and leaving only prolongs incubation, delaying the time when the eggs start to hatch.

When a female leaves her eggs temporarily, the male stands by the nest box or sometimes enters the box for short periods. When perching outside the box, he watches for predators and tries enticing the female to come back and start incubating. A male doing this appears apprehensive and agitated. Perching on the nest box, he will wave his wings, showing his blue wings and back to the female. He may also cling to the entrance hole, poking his head in and out to show her where he wants her to be. This will continue until the female enters the cavity and incubates again.

When the female is back inside, she will often adjust or gently turn her eggs before sitting down. This is thought to help the eggs warm evenly and prevent the inner membranes from sticking to the shells. She may also rearrange the nesting material, making minor adjustments to the grass.

At night the male might rest in the nest cavity with the female, but usually he will sit off to the side. Some males spend the night in a cavity nearby, or on a tree branch or shrub. Much of this depends on the weather and the individual male.

Average incubation time for the Eastern Bluebird is 12–14 days. Early in spring when temperatures are cooler, incubation takes longer. Later in the season, the process can be as much as a day shorter. The range of incubation for Eastern Bluebirds is slightly longer, 12–18 days. Like Eastern Bluebirds, Western Bluebirds incubate 12–14 days, but they have a shorter range of 12–17 days. Mountain Bluebirds average slightly longer, 13–15 days, but they have an even shorter range, 12–16 days.

Along with temperature, the amount of food the male feeds an incubating female also influences how long it takes before the eggs start to hatch. One study showed that when a female was fed only once in a while, she sat on her eggs for just 25 minutes at a time. With more feedings she stayed on the eggs 40 minutes, and with constant feeding she incubated for over an hour. A male feeding a mother bird more often allows her to incubate more consistently, shortening her time on the job.

Incubation is simply not a fixed process. With variables differing greatly from year to year and female to female, it seems amazing that the eggs hatch at all.

HATCHING

Hatching takes the better part of a day to a day or more and often occurs in the order of first egg laid to last. Timing depends on when incubation started, whether or not the eggs were equally warmed and their position in the nest. One study showed that while the majority of eggs hatch within a couple hours of sunrise, they can hatch anytime of day. Some clutches of eggs hatch simultaneously, each taking only an hour or so. Other clutches take 24 hours or more for all eggs to hatch.

Baby birds scrape their way out of the egg with the aid of an egg tooth, which is a hardened tip at the end of the upper bill. Using specialized neck muscles, chicks rub their egg tooth against the inside of the eggshell, creating a weak spot through which they break free. The egg tooth drops off or is reabsorbed in the bill within 24 hours of hatching.

Young bluebirds start out like most other baby songbirds—blind (eyes sealed shut), naked and helpless. This condition is called altricial. Precocial chicks, such as ducklings and goslings, are covered with feathers at hatching and can leave the nest within hours. Hatching takes a lot of energy, and often a chick will lie in complete exhaustion for a while after emerging from the egg. This is a critical time in the life of a baby bird.

The parents usually remove eggshells and drop them some distance from the nest cavity, a practice that supposedly keeps predators from being attracted to the nest. Like many other birds, the mother will eat some of the eggshells. This behavior results in replenishment of the calcium and other nutrients she lost during reproduction.

While the chicks grow, infertile eggs remain in the nest. Some parents are able to remove them—others are not. Young nestlings that die in the nest are often removed by the parents, who drag the dead by the wing or leg to the nest entrance for disposal. One study showed that adult birds can move lifeless chicks weighing up to 10 grams.

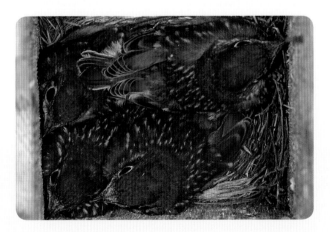

BROODING

For several days after the chicks hatch, the mother bluebird sits on her young to warm them in much the same way she did to incubate her eggs. This process is called brooding. Initially, chicks not only lack feathers to keep them warm, their thermoregulatory system is nonfunctional. This means newly hatched chicks cannot maintain their body core temperature, and that makes brooding by the mother a necessity.

In warmer weather, the mother doesn't need to brood as much as she would in cooler temperatures. When it's chilly and damp, chicks may quickly become too weak to lift their heads to feed. Cold, wet spring weather is the primary killer of young bluebirds and other baby birds. It takes much longer for parent birds to find food in chilly rain because insects are inactive. The longer the parents are away from the nest, the colder and weaker their chicks become. When baby birds get too feeble to lift their heads, they can't feed, frailty increases, and this downward cycle accelerates rapidly. Before long, the fading young expire.

It takes approximately 5 days for Eastern Bluebird chicks to grow enough feathers to maintain their body temperature. The same process takes about 6 days for Mountain Bluebird chicks. In Western Bluebird chicks it takes even longer—around 8 days.

FEEDING THE CHICKS

Both bluebird parents feed their young birds. Although Eastern Bluebird males do the most hunting and feeding of young, the females also bring food in on a regular basis. Some studies show that Western Bluebird females feed the young more often than the male.

Baby birds are so small and weak during the first few days of life, feeding is not intense and food items are small. After about 6 days, feeding greatly increases and food items get larger.

Once a morsel is swallowed, a chick immediately turns, raises its bottom and exposes its cloaca, the opening from which small, individual sacs of fecal material are excreted. For the first 5–6 days, parents gently grab fecal sacs and eat them. When the chicks are older, parents take the sacs and fly off, depositing them on branches or other objects well away from the nest. This keeps the interior of the cavity and the baby birds sanitary.

Without peeking inside the nest cavity, some people try to approximate the age of nestlings simply by observing parental feeding activities. When chicks are under 6 days of age, parents enter the nest cavity and leave without a fecal sac. Parents of chicks that are 6–12 days old enter the cavity with larger food items and leave with fecal sacs in their bills. When chicks reach 12–18 days, parents merely stop at the entrance hole and poke their heads inside the cavity to deliver food and remove fecal sacs.

Eastern Bluebirds usually feed their young a diet of insects. Rarely, an overly ambitious male bluebird captures and delivers small frogs and other unusual food to the young.

HATCHLINGS DAY BY DAY

Newly hatched young are mostly pink and rather funny looking—with only a few downy feathers on their heads and backs, it appears as if they are sporting fuzzy Mohawks. Their eyes are sealed shut, and they can't move except to lift their heads and open their beaks.

By 2–3 days of age, their size has more than doubled and dark spots have developed on their bodies and wings. Most of the growth at this time is drawing from reserve nutrition that accumulated from the egg yolk—there's not much feeding going on by the parents yet.

After 3–4 days, the wings darken due to developing feathers just under the skin. At 5–6 days, feathers with some blue begin breaking through the skin. These are called pin feathers because they resemble pins sticking out of the birds.

The inside of a bluebird chick's mouth is bright yellow with a yellow rim. An open mouth of this color is thought to act like a target on which parents place the food. By day 7, chicks are feeding vigorously and their eyes are starting to open.

Once the feathers start emerging, growth goes into fast forward. Eyes open completely by day 8, feathers unsheathe and the chicks begin to preen. By 9–10 days, the young are three-quarters the size of adults and covered with a full coat of feathers. While they don't look like adults yet, they are well on their way to flying. At this time the sex of young birds may be determined by wing color. Young males have bright blue wings; females don't.

The young are fully active in the nest, stretching their wings and preening regularly when they reach 12–15 days. By now their white eye-rings are also starting to appear. During days 16–17, the young are peeking out of the cavity entrance and parents are perching on the nest box, calling to them.

Contrary to popular belief, bluebird parents don't withhold food to encourage the young to leave. With larger, more nutritious prey items brought in, feedings become less frequent by 18 days, and the hatchlings know it is time to move out. They have outgrown the nest cavity, and the nesting materials are flattened from their weight. One by one they perch at the entrance hole and launch into the world of flight. Once they leave the nest cavity, they never return. At this stage they are called fledglings.

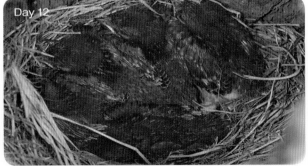

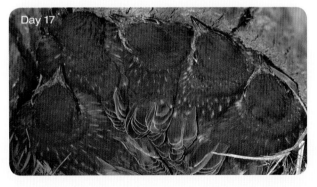

Most young bluebirds usually leave the nest, or fledge, between 15–18 days of age. Bluebird fledglings—light gray birds with white spots and yellow "lips"—are surprisingly small and light. Over the next week or so, they may spend a couple hours to an entire day on the ground, where their parents follow them around, delivering food. Others perch in a tree or shrub and call to their parents. When adults land nearby, the fledglings beg, opening their beaks for food and quivering their wings. They often stay near each other and sometimes line up to spend the night together, sharing warmth as they did in the nest cavity.

TAKING FLIGHT

The young are not taught to fly—this ability is seemingly "hard-wired" into the birds. They want to fly in the same way our toddlers want to walk, doing it on their own when they are ready. The first flights are often short and direct, usually to a nearby tree or shrub. If a perch is not close, they just land on the ground—which makes them easy prey for domestic cats and dogs. When a family gets separated, the young may give plaintive calls at regular intervals to signal their position, to which the parents respond, bringing something to eat.

This is also the time when some well-meaning people think young birds are orphaned or deserted and erroneously rescue them. Unless you see both adult birds dead, the young are not abandoned—they're just waiting for their parents to return from hunting.

About 7–10 days after fledging, the young start following their parents around and constantly beg for food. This causes them to fly more often, which strengthens their flight muscles. Most of the feeding is done by the male, especially if the female is constructing a new nest. At around 10–14 days after fledging, the young are finding and catching a few things to eat. About 3 weeks after leaving the nest, they are finding more food on their own, supplementing the prey items brought in by their parents.

INDEPENDENCE

At around 5–6 weeks of age, fledglings are honing their hunting skills, dropping out of trees and other perches onto insects on the ground, and flying out to capture insects in the air. During this time, parents gradually stop feeding.

Young birds often stay in the general area after becoming independent. There are some reports of young first brood birds coming back to help feed the second brood, or even the third. Known as helpers, these birds have not reached breeding age, but apparently have the instincts to care for and feed begging young. This behavior is seen in all three bluebird species, but is most common in Western Bluebirds.

SECOND FAMILIES

Within days after the first brood fledges, the male takes over most of the feeding duties while the female builds a nest for her second batch of eggs. When another cavity is available nearby, the female will usually make the new residence there. Some females construct the second nest elsewhere while the first brood is still in the cavity. Others use the original nest, replacing most of the old nesting material with a fresh supply of dried grass.

When a female lays 5 eggs in the first nest, she will sometimes produce only 4 or maybe 3 eggs the second time. The decrease may be because the amount of calcium required for egg production is taxing her body. Others think since the end of breeding season is getting closer, fewer eggs speeds the hatching process.

THIRD BROODS

Depending on weather, the health of the adult birds, the food supply and other factors, a pair of bluebirds may even produce a third batch of eggs in one season. This is not very common in northern states due to the length of the breeding season. In southern states it often gets too hot for a third brood. Bluebirds don't breed during winter.

Studies show that bluebirds with a failed first nest try again about 30–50 percent of the time. Successful pairs renest 75-85 percent of the time. Pairs that have successful nests remain together between seasons and during migration. This behavior is fairly unique to bluebirds, being uncommon in most songbirds. There is a good chance that if two bluebirds were successful partners, both will return the following year to set up shop and get down to the business of raising more young.

Surprisingly, the life of an adult bluebird after breeding season is fairly relaxing. Studies show that between 55–75 percent of an adult bluebird's day is spent resting or in relative inactivity that may include sleeping. Hunting constitutes only 5–10 percent of the day.

Rest breaks are usually taken high in a tree or on a favorite perch. An adult will spread one wing over its back and tuck in its beak, resting its head on a shoulder (scapula). Sometimes a bluebird will tuck one foot up into its feathers while balancing on the other, which is the standard position for most resting birds. Bluebirds at rest during cold spells will fluff their feathers to keep warm. Birds under 13 days of age sleep with their heads dropped or hanging down.

By the end of breeding season and summer, bluebird behavior changes dramatically. While at first territorial and aggressive toward other bluebirds, they are now becoming more gregarious and congenial. Both close and distant family members gather to form large flocks ranging from 10–50 birds, with some flocks numbering in the hundreds.

Flocks migrating south from northern states gather in October and November, although when these birds leave often depends on the weather. Warblers, grosbeaks, hummingbirds and other species leave the same time every year no matter what. Bluebirds, however, usually stick around well into early winter if the weather is mild and there is no snow cover. When winter comes earlier, they migrate earlier. In most years, bluebirds can be seen well into November, even in the most northern states. In the South, bluebirds may not migrate at all. The same is true for Mountain Bluebirds in western states. These birds form large flocks with northern migrants and remain in the area.

WINTER DIET

While the bluebird diet in spring and summer consists mainly of insects, come fall, the number of insects drops dramatically. With this, the diet changes and bluebirds start feeding in groups. One study showed 85–90 percent of the winter diet is berries. During winter, a bluebird group will descend on a fruit source, such as crab apples or sumac, and eat until satisfied or the supply is exhausted. Other sources of nutrition in late fall and early winter are dormant insect eggs. When the food runs low, the birds move on to search for new sources, usually south.

Surviving cold winter nights is a challenge for any bird. One way bluebirds increase their chances of making it to another day is by remaining in groups and roosting communally in cavities. In warmer weather, bluebirds roost alone in cavities or other sheltered areas. During winter, when temperatures dip below freezing, bluebirds seek the added warmth of other roosting bluebirds to share body heat. Bluebirds appear to prefer natural cavities over nest boxes for roosting, perhaps because they tend to be larger, but they will use both for warmth and shelter. Groups may stay together all winter.

Sometimes bluebirds will perch on nest boxes during winter and peek inside. Don't confuse this curiosity with out-of-season nesting behavior—these birds are just checking things out.

The return of bluebirds in springtime has inspired people for hundreds of years. Song writers, poets and more have been moved to artistic creativity just by the sight and sound of this most wonderful of thrushes. There is something grounding in the regular rhythm of changing seasons and the migration of birds.

While the bluebird was nearly driven to extinction by people, it also recovered by the human hand that contributed to its demise. Thousands of individuals across America have spent their hard-earned cash on building supplies for nest boxes, donated their time to educate the public and offered food to the birds—all in efforts to save the beloved bluebird species.

Throughout our country, nature enthusiasts have not only assembled, installed and maintained bluebird trails, they have spent countless hours monitoring and caring for the beautiful blue occupants. Bluebird monitors gathering at annual conferences exchange information about being even better stewards of the birds of blue. All of these people are truly dedicated to the conservation of a remarkable songbird species, the bluebird.

BLUEBIRD RECOVERY PROGRAM

The recovery of the bluebird is a shining example of what can happen when ordinary people work together to save a species. Bluebird populations across the country had declined for about 80 years and it was estimated that 90 percent of the total population had been eliminated. In some places it had been completely wiped out. Concerned by the possibility that bluebirds could become extinct everywhere, individuals and groups started taking action to help all three bluebird species recover.

The key to this remarkable recovery has been the volunteers—the people who gave and who continue to give hundreds to thousands of hours of their time not only to learn more about bluebirds, but to construct and install nest boxes and form official organizations. To promote bluebirds, these organizations presented educational workshops to the public, built bluebird boxes to give away and sponsored bluebird trails. Through their efforts, more people became bluebird enthusiasts and more nest boxes were built and installed.

Nearly every state in the nation, along with Canada, now has an official organization devoted exclusively to helping bluebirds. In addition, a national bluebird organization, North American Bluebird Society (NABS), lists all state affiliates online (www.nabluebirdsociety.org). These nonprofit organizations are dedicated to education, conservation and research. Supporting the organizations with your membership fee is a wonderful way to start learning more about bluebirds and contributing to bluebird recovery.

No other scientific field relies on citizen science more than the bluebird community. Through citizen observations and research, many organizations have made substantial contributions to the body of knowledge about bluebirds. Society members, many without scientific backgrounds, are monitoring bluebird behaviors and conducting research in various areas of interest such as breeding habits, nest cavity success, sparrow and swallow species control, predator guard effectiveness and more.

The volume of data accumulated by volunteer nest box monitors is unprecedented. Combining this with other databases and access to the Internet, knowledge once shared by only a few researchers is now accessible to millions. This has made possible the great recovery of our beloved bluebird.

Placing nest boxes along a bluebird trail is a commitment in time and effort.

Bluebird Trail Checklist

- Get permission from the property owner or manager to start a bluebird trail

- Choose a convenient, easily accessible place for monitoring

- Select open habitat, such as a pasture, rural road, old field, golf course, cemetery, park or yard, that has several trees, stumps or man-made objects where bluebirds can perch and hunt; place at least 100 feet from the edge of woods and avoid places where pesticides are used

- Mount the nest box on a metal pole, using $^3/_4$" electrical conduit or other smooth metal to prevent predators from climbing to the box, or attach the box to a wooden pole and install a predator guard

- Position the box at a height where the interior can be easily viewed, about 4–5 feet off the ground

- Install pairs of boxes about 20–40 feet apart to reduce competition for nest cavities and place each nest box pair 50–100 yards apart

NEST BOX STYLES

There are many wonderful nest box designs available for purchase or construction. Most are made from wood or plastic. Others may simply be hollow gourds. Some are easier to mount on metal poles, while others offer more predator control. Some are well suited for cold spring weather and some work better in hot weather. Choose the best kind for your location and needs. Here are a few common examples to consider:

- Peterson Nest Box – front opening with a slanted roof

- NABS Eastern or Western Bluebird Nest Box – side opening with a slanted roof

- Gilbertson PVC Nest Box – round PVC with a flat wooden top

- Chalet Nest Box – pitched roof and side opening

- Square box with a flat roof and modified entrance hole just under the roof on the front

- Materials – ³/₄" cedar wood or PVC plastic

- Entrance – 1¹/₂" round hole or 1³/₈" by 2¹/₄" oval hole

- Floor Area – 4" by 4" square or 4" diameter

- Monitor Access – door that swings open but does not disturb the nest

- Color – natural wood or light-colored paint to minimize overheating

- Waterproofing / Drainage – ample roof that covers the structure and keeps water out; drainage holes in floor; vent hole or slots on walls near the top to allow excess heat to escape

- Perches – none

Gilbertson

NABS

ABOUT THE AUTHOR

Naturalist, wildlife photographer and writer Stan Tekiela is the originator of the popular nature appreciation book series that includes loons, eagles, bluebirds, owls, hummingbirds, woodpeckers and wolves. For over two decades, Stan has authored more than 100 field guides and wildlife audio CDs for nearly every state in the nation, presenting many species of birds, mammals, reptiles and amphibians, trees, wildflowers and cacti. Holding a Bachelor of Science degree in Natural History from the University of Minnesota and as an active professional naturalist for more than 20 years, Stan studies and photographs wildlife throughout the United States and has received various national and regional awards for his books and photographs. Also a well-known columnist and radio personality, his syndicated column appears in more than 20 newspapers and his wildlife programs are broadcast on a number of Midwest radio stations. He is a member of the North American Nature Photography Association and Canon Professional Services. Stan lives in Victoria, Minnesota, with his wife, Katherine, and daughter, Abigail. He can be contacted via his web page at www.naturesmart.com.